It Starts Like This

Shelby Leigh © 2016

ISBN: 1535597666
ISBN-13: 978-1535597661

Contents

It Starts Like This

I remember those nights I awoke from nightmares, my sheets damp from sweat yet my body shivered like I had just finished an ice bath. My teeth would chatter and I'd scan my bedroom for the monsters, finding crazy-shaped heads in the shadows and green eyes peeking out between the tiny slits of my closed closet doors.

I would slowly, carefully step out of bed so as not to wake them and sprint to my parent's bedroom telling my seven-year-old self, *don't look back.* I would traipse over to my parent's bed and squirm in between them, and it was in the warmth of familiar faces that I could fall asleep within seconds.

But something changes when you get older. I've learned monsters are not shadows in the dark nor are they nightmares that disappear when the sun rises. You can't just wake up and find yourself back in your own bed anymore. They are within you and they are wherever you look. You may even get a better night's sleep now because seven hours of closed eyes means seven hours of escape.

But don't push the monsters away. Let them free. Let them out of your mind, your blood, your bones. Write.

Wide Awake

Don't get me wrong, I'm an independent person.
But I quite like the idea of waking up in the middle
of the night with your arm wrapped around me.
Not protecting me, just holding me.

And when I can't sleep, I get to admire you.
I can hold my breath until our heart beats are in
sync or maybe I can kiss the scar above your lip.
I can count the freckles on your arms like I am an
astronomer mesmerized by the stars in the sky.
I can guess where your dreams are taking you by
studying your wavering smile or fluttering eyes.

And when I do fall asleep, I will dream about you,
the last thing my eyes saw
before I gave in to the exhaustion.

And when I wake up, the first thing I will see is
you.
Maybe you will still be sleeping soundly
holding onto me,
or maybe I will catch you admiring me, too.

Her

Admire her.
Notice the crinkles that outline
her eyes like a crescent moon
when she smiles.
Watch how she giggles
or plays with her hands
when she's proud.

Touch her.
Prove to her that the stretch marks
decorating her skin
are intricate works of art.
Caress her with gentle hands and
soft fingertips, admiring
every curve of her body.

Cherish her.
Adore her.
Love her.

After all, she's the one who taught you how.

Battle Scars

I can create a painting
from the freckles on your cheeks
or a song from your soft breaths on my neck
I can trace the scars on your thighs
with our legs intertwined
a mark of triumph not of failure
a memory of a war you fought with yourself
and won

The Thief

I think you accidentally
stole my heart

keep it

you'll probably
treat it better
than I do anyway

You

I am in love with your sleepy voice and crooked smile.
I am in love with your passion, for me and for life.
I am in love with your wisdom, gained from what has been lost and what is to come.
I am in love with the soft curls of your hair and dark hazel eyes.
I am in love with your sensitivity, your drive to always do better and be better.
I am in love with how you take me for who I am.
I am in love with your romantic side and with your serious side.
I am in love with the comfort you emit, your ability to be my home when you're a thousand miles away.
I am in love with how you look at me.
I am in love with your motivation and your support for my silly dreams.
I am in love with your accessibility, my shoulder to cry on, my protector at three a.m. when I have nowhere else to turn.

And I am in love with the way you love me.

Swearing

I swear
with every kiss
you leave words on my tongue
and every time you break away
I breathe a poem
into my lungs

Dew

think of me as a rose
blooming
underneath the hot sun
curling my stem
towards you
and baring my soul

every part of me
that is beautiful
you will not see
until I am ready to
show you
unwrapping

my most private
thoughts and
letting them escape
in the wind's caress
only to drown
in dewy grass

Warm Blankets

wrap me up
in the sounds of your laugh
that comfort me more
than the warmest blanket
and soothe me greater
than a hot water bath

I am fragile
in the strong gates
of your arms
and I fear I will crumble
to pieces in your grasp
but then you laugh

and I am no longer afraid
not of you
because how could
an iron statue
carry the voice of an
angel on its shoulders?

Keepsakes

if you lend me your heart
I vow to not break it
I'll keep it safe within mine
so no one can take it

and if ever you are lost
with nowhere to roam
reach for my hand
and I'll guide you home

You Are Like Poetry

You are like poetry.
The thin lines decorating your hands
are the black ink that marks a lined page.
The beat of your heart is
a steady stream of words
with perfect rhythm.
You are the words I breathe
and the rhymes I arrange
and the ink flowing out of my pen.
You are the thoughts in my head
that I put down on paper.
You are the everlasting memories
that words create.
You are permanent
and beautiful
and mine.

Laughter

I have never known a sweeter sound
than your laughter
maybe they are right when they say
laughter is the best medicine
because when I hear that glorious sound
my sadness melts away
like a spoonful of sugar on my tongue
and I am sure that if I heard
your laugh everyday
I could never be unhappy again

Rhythm

tonight
you fell asleep on my chest
and I became conscious
of every breath

watching your head rise and fall
and feeling so loved
that you trusted me
with such an innocent task
of being your resting place
your home for slumber

and I will slow my heart's rhythm
so you can focus on your dreams
and if a nightmare creeps
into your mind
just open your eyes
and feel my heart beating close to yours

Homeless

I made a home in your arms
carved your collarbone to
perfectly rest my head
slowed your heartbeat
so I could fall asleep to
the sound of soft footsteps
laid your arms tightly around
my waist so I would always
feel safe no matter where my
dreams took me

I made a home in your arms
and I don't know what changed
but you began showing up
in my nightmares
and my head no longer fit
in the delicate curve of your neck
and I awoke to find
you had pushed me aside
and were sleeping soundly
as I wiped my tears dry

Wishes

I pretend the crescent moon
is the soft curve of your back
and the stars are the twinkle
in your eyes when you smile

I pretend the crickets chirp to the
tempo of your heart beating
and the tree branches swaying
are your hips as we dance

I pretend the shooting star
I just wished upon
will hear my plea and you
will soon be back in my arms again

Blank Page

I want to stop writing poetry about you
but my pen does not obey
as soon as the ink touches a blank page
words appear I never wished to say
I tried to write a poem about
spring beginning to bloom
but it ended up as a haiku
about me missing you

Blue

I'm standing before you
a stranger that I used to know
the sunlight
streaming through
closed flowered curtains
casts a shadow on your face
so I can only see
tear-stained eyes
pleading for another chance
and
I don't remember them being
so blue

Dust Storm

you are the blur in my eyes
that comes from staring at the sun too long,
and your fading light drowns me in sorrow
as you disappear beneath the horizon.
My eyes sting like I've been caught in a dust storm
and my tears burn as they crawl down my face
as if I'm being branded by your desertion.
But then--
a glimmer of hope--
like a ray of light pushing through
a dark cloud
you turn around and shoot me
in the heart with beaming eyes
like lasers
and I am bleeding.
I never understood the term
'broken heart' until this moment,
until I am lying on my back
staring up at the sky
desperately looking for a
glimpse of you in the clouds

Sleepwalker

I am sleepwalking through a forest
where minutes soon become hours
branches tap me on the shoulder
and sunlight creeps behind me
as dawn breaks to say hello
and your silhouette becomes
a shadow
staring at me as sunlight
pierces black eyes
I take a step closer as you take a step back
that's how it has always been
I laugh
and your silhouette becomes
a shadow
I blink
and you are gone

Predator

it was her walk that destroyed me
the confidence in her stride
eyes that read every inch of my body
in one glance

it was her eyes that stripped me
of my own self-love
the disgust on her face reaching
through my skin to the bone

it was her smile that melted me
a half-moon upon bitter lips
a pitying shake of the head
that molded me into a beggar

it was her hair that captured me
dark brown rope circling around my body
like a snake attacking its prey
and I was hers for the taking

Mountain Song

I can shout how I feel
to the mountains
but my voice will not echo like it should
and so I will write it down
in black ink,
a permanence you cannot erase when
you stop loving me
and the mountains
forget the song I sang for you
when I stood on top of the world

Poison

your name was always
my favorite song to sing
and when you said mine
my heart stopped beating

the way it rolled off your tongue
coated in sugar and a smile
it's funny how
I never tasted the poison
until you kissed me

Erosion

your words pierce my lungs
like nails scraping down a chalkboard
burying themselves in my veins
and leaving scratches on my skin
I try to run from your voice
but sound travels faster than my feet
and besides,
every time I close my eyes
your voice is all I hear
echoing through my brain
like you are standing on top of a mountain
shouting to me at the bottom of a canyon
and I am surrounded by rock walls that have
been perfectly eroding for centuries
making way for you to dig my grave

Thoughts

I always had an easy time writing
about people and places and things.
I never struggled with conveying my thoughts
through words and
I would sit down to a new sheet of paper
and watch words escape my pen
quicker than thoughts
ran through my head.
But when I met you,
I stopped writing.
I couldn't find the words
to say how I felt
and for a while I told myself
it was because I was too happy
and you were too special
to be limited to just words.
But then
I realized something as I picked up
my pen for the first time in months–
you took the words out of me
because there were none in you.

Close

Isn't it strange how
someone across the sea can
make you feel so close
yet you can look into
a person's eyes and they
still feel miles away?
That's how I felt
when I looked at you.
I could see the blue
in your eyes so clearly,
the dark eyelashes
and the crinkle lines
but I had no idea what you
were looking for.

I just knew it wasn't me.

Fears

I fear the night
the kind of pitch black
where even shadows
disappear
I fear the quiet,
the thumping
of my own heart
amidst utter silence

but
I fear you
most of all
for how quickly
you became a stranger
when once
you were my closest
friend

The Dagger

I thought I knew you better than anyone
but even I could not see your sword
plunging straight into my heart and
now I am paranoid
that he will hurt me like you did
I have lost the ability to open my arms
for someone else to hold because
every time I do
I await another dagger
to break the scar that has finally healed

Bones

and if you only knew
how my bones ache for you
I wonder if you'd tell me
your body is fragile, too

Spinning

Closing your eyes and feeling your mind
swirl through a desert of darkness
like your imagination is parched and
needs something new to quench its thirst and
so you can feel
behind closed eyes
your mind searching through many worlds
much too quickly for comprehension and
everything looks familiar yet
you do not have time to place it
before you are onto the next thing and
then the next and
when your brain finally catches up to your
imagination
your head is spinning and
you can't wait to do it all over again because
at long last you feel free,
like you are in charge of any world you create
and your mind does not stop until every last detail
is down on paper.

That is how it feels to write.

Ashes, Ashes

I decided to
forget you today
so I ripped the pages
from my journal
that were about you
and tossed them in a fire

I watched
red and orange flames
curl around each page
consuming words
I thought I could never surrender
to a pile of dust and ash

We All Fall Down

you carried me gently in your hand
a pocket-sized disciple
nestled within the intricate lines on your palm

I was easy to love and so you loved me
and wherever you walked
I was sure to follow

and you knew that all too well
because you walked straight for a cliff
and stopped at the edge

and watched me tumble
down
       down
             down
to where all your other followers lay

Rhymes

I fell for you
the way most writers do
admiring small details
and poorly written haikus

people will think it's fiction
that I felt you in my veins
when my blood turned to ink
and you still consumed my brain

I filled up each and every page
with all my love for you
but when the words ran out
it seems your love did too

Message in a Bottle

I sent you a letter today
written with your favorite pen
you'll have to excuse the smudges
you know I write with my left hand

I folded the page in thirds and
scrawled your name across the top
I tried not to make it sappy
but once I began I could not stop

I placed it in a bottle and
pushed the cork on tight and
I walked down to the beach
in the middle of the night

I watched it float in the water
before the waves took it away
here's hoping someone out there
will read the words I had to say

Hidden

come and find me
in the corners of your mind
hiding in the ink of your pen
I am words
waiting to be spilled out
between the lines of a page
I am emotions
you have suppressed
and details you don't
even know exist
but you will remember
if you just try
press your pen against
a blank page
and I will handle the rest

Mona

I painted her on a canvas
an etched permanence

though time will pass
her beauty will remain

at the tip of a paintbrush
poignant and moving

slowly as to remember
every detail

of raised eyebrows
and nimble fingers

silently drowning
behind upturned lips

see the faint trace of a smile
if you lean in close

Empty

he just can't let her go
it's not the sound of her laugh
or the softness of her skin
that he misses most
it's the way she loved him
like no one ever has
the way she held him
when he was hurting her
the way she felt his pain
like it was her own
and he just wasn't ready
to let all of that go

yet this morning
he opened his eyes
and she was gone

Clichés

I know it's cliché to say
you were like a drug
and I became addicted to you,
that your lips tasted like
bitter ecstasy,
that I knew it was wrong
yet I always wanted more,
that your whiskey-colored eyes
hypnotized me
and I felt knots in my stomach
if I looked away

maybe it's wrong to say
that you were my drug
and I was addicted to you
like the nicotine
in my first cigarette
that buried me with its
glowing embers and
acrid smoke
so I won't say it
I'll only say I never thought
I could live a day without you

yet today I opened my eyes
and I have never felt more alive

Journal

once I sculpted you out of letters
and carved quotes into your skin
you became every word
I wanted someone to tell me
even if you said it with silence
you let me spill tears on your shoulder
even though it left a stain
and you never forgot a single detail
while I poured my heart out every day
yet I abandoned you as I always do
when you ran out of space for me
and I realized as I tucked you
behind rows of books on my shelves
that you never asked for my eyes
to spill tears on your corners
and my mind to drip words on each line
I ruined my creation,
my sculpture born of ink,
until I had no more tears left to cry

Shadow

I promise the sun will still shine tomorrow
as bright as every day
and the clouds will cast a shadow
that looks just like your outline
so I'll stand straight within your silhouette,
pretending you were never gone
until dusk comes and
the sun sinks below the horizon
and your shadow
disappears for one more night

Daydreaming

sometimes I study the rain
I think about their journey from the clouds
and I wonder if they are scared
like I am scared
and I wonder if other people
see these things
as I do

especially you

I wonder if you think about the rain
and I wonder if you still think about me

Dust

when did you turn to dust
gently soaring through the air
hiding in the glare of sunlight
and forging a home on every surface

what were you before you were ash
burning on a stone hearth
a remembrance of the unknown
a reminder of the words you've burned

who were you before you were broken
when your dreams still opened your eyes
and you danced through each day on tiptoes
and broke through even the darkest shadows

Missing

the earth
never knew what
it was missing until
you came along

and too soon
the sky grew envious
of the land
on which you walked

and so heaven
opened its gates
and took you away
from me

Mirror, Mirror

I saw her once
in a reflection
the one that used to be me
I barely recognized her
with eyes full of life
and a smile that grazed
her cheeks

when did I stop
loving her
the one that used to be me
a mirage in the mirror
reaching out
with soft fingertips
and a spirit so carefree

and just like that she
disappears
a tangible memory
of what I used to be
before I stopped loving myself
and my smile faded
and I never set myself free

Scrapes

I am ashamed for
saying I want you to fall
like I fell for you
but when you do,
and you will,
you'll scrape your knees and
dirty your jeans
and do anything to be hers
and you'll finally understand
why it was so hard
for me to unravel my fingers
from yours
and watch the wind
carry you away from me

Colors

my mouth burns after you kiss me
and I don't know what that means
because I thought I loved you

the sky turns blue, orange, scarlet
reflecting off the white snow
in which my toes are buried

my body is shivering and cold
but there is fire on my tongue
and in the dead of winter

after you kiss me
I stand in the numb air exhaling the
smoke you breathed into my lungs

Sting

it stings between my fingers
the weathered spots on my skin
where his hands used to live
and every time I think of him
the pain sharpens
and I can feel it on my hands
my neck
my shoulders
my heart

every place he once touched me
he made sure to leave a scar

Half Empty

now the glass is half full
it is sitting on the counter
sweating down its sides
my fingers curl around it
leaving prints on the glass
and it meets my parted lips

now the glass is half empty
and my breath fogs up the sides
and I fear I will see
my own reflection
if I look too close
so my hands let go

now the glass is empty
shattered
I am surrounded by
thousands of fragments
and in each one there
is a reflection of me

I pick up the pieces
that slice the tips of my fingers
and I apologize for
my own destruction
for it is no one's fault
that I fear my own reflection

Sightings

the rain is falling so fast
that my vision is blurry
but I think
I saw
a glimpse of you
turning the corner

it's funny
you know
how quickly my life changed
from seeing you everyday
to crossing my fingers
hoping

each time I go outside
I would
perhaps
be lucky enough
to see you
if only for a moment

Untouched

I am surrounded by people
and no one to talk to
I am a brown leaf
in a pile of red and orange
unnoticed and untouched
but look closely and you will see
the hints of color that I once was
before I fell to the ground
and lay there
waiting for someone to pick me up
and admire me
only me
and bring me along
clutched softly
in the palm of their hand

Books

surrounded by old books
with withered yellow pages
curled around my finger

that is my favorite place to be
silently I wonder who has read their words
who has cried and who has laughed

which stains are tears and which are spilled tea
crisp pages torn from delicate binding
yet the words do not stray

and I am entranced by
the infinite worlds I can create
from a single page

Clueless

I laugh when I think about you
having no clue that your words
still slice through my ears
and reverberate through my skull
how you sleep soundly at the dead of night
sprawled out under a blanket of silence
while I drift off to the soothing
pain of sobs escaping my lips

And so I laugh while I carve poetry
out of the pieces of my heart
that were left on the ground
and though you were the one who
placed them there I must
thank you for stepping carefully
over them on your way out
so the pieces did not shatter

Heart and Soul

after all this time
I thought it was just my heart
that hurt and
could be broken
but today I felt something
deeper
behind my heart
and my lungs

I think maybe
it was my soul

it started as a dull ache
in my ribs
and tightened my lungs
so my breaths became short
and then I swear
I felt you in my body
knocking on my heart
as if to say

I'm never letting
you go

Full Moon

today I noticed I am a lot
like the moon
ignored and unexplored when
I am barely there
just a sliver in the darkness

but when I am at my best
full and vibrant
that is when I am noticed
that is when the wolves howl
to feel alive

Symphony

whoever says silence is not a sound
has never been alone for so long
that they write a song to the
beat of their own heart
or memorize the
rhythm of their breathing

only then
amidst utter silence
can you close your eyes
and hear a symphony

Words

when my heart aches
it's words that pour out
not blood
and these words
are more powerful than
the sharpest sword
they are carved
by desire
and anger
but have more beauty than
the largest pearl
like blood
however
they stain every surface
they touch
breathing life into all
who will listen

Echo

I hear your name in every sound
but you are the loudest
when the wind blows
howling your name into the humid air
and spinning up
to the treetops

and the birds in their nests
echo the air
and the branches stir
waving hello to you
wherever you are

Shelby Leigh

Seawater

you erected a home among
the shadows of people long gone
and now you wait each day

for the sun to rise so you can
free yourself from the confinement
of her haunting silhouette

and you dream of seawater washing
over her footprints in the sand
so you don't have to step in them

why are you living in an echo
when you are so much more
than the words spoken before you

why are you living in your scars
when you have the power
to watch them heal before your eyes

Mold

my mind yearned for something greater
than what I could see
with my own eyes
and every day I thought
there was something wrong with me
because I was not happy in this life

my mind yearned for something greater
than this constant cycle of hate
but as far as my eyes can see
we live in a world
where people aren't people
until they fit your perfect mold

Passion

because all it takes
is passion,
passion that burns
like an everlasting candle
in your soul
that is the first thing
you think of when you wake up
and the last thing you remember
as you drift asleep

if it burns out,
this does not mean
you are not passionate —
your candle just encountered
a gust of wind
and is ready to be lit again
when you are ready
for its glow

See You Soon

I remember sitting at the kitchen table
practicing my writing.
My little left hand grasped a pen
and I proudly showed off my cursive to you,
watching the admiring, toothless smile on your
face.

I remember walking by you on the couch
thinking you were asleep.
I tip-toed past only to find you were tricking me.
You grabbed me and held me up
before I fell to the ground in a fit of laughter.

I remember being in awe that you
could carry me with your eighty-year-old bones.

I remember the jokes
and the choking fits
and the hospital visits
and sitting in the front row at church
watching my mom dab the tears in her eyes.

I remember the reception and the blurred vision
when I wasn't sure if I was laughing or crying
at the stories people shared of you.

I remember going home that day feeling empty
but knowing you're better off,
wherever you are.

A Reminder

remember that sometimes
it's ok to close your eyes
and forget the world,
to think for yourself,
breathe deeply,
and do that one thing
you've been putting off
for months
and when you are ready
to view the world with
new-born eyes,
you will find that
the stars still shine,
the waves still crash,
the sun still rises,
and
your heart still beats.

It Ends Like This

yesterday I woke up tired
it hurt to open my eyes
and so I went back to sleep
and when I woke up again
the sun was disappearing
and I lived in the darkness

today I woke up sad
but I pushed myself to
get up and get dressed
and it hurt at first
but then I smiled at the sun
and I walked in its rays

tomorrow I'll wake up happy
and if not tomorrow
then maybe the next day
or maybe it will take me
a week or a month
but I'll get there